TRICKS, TRAPS, AND TOOLS

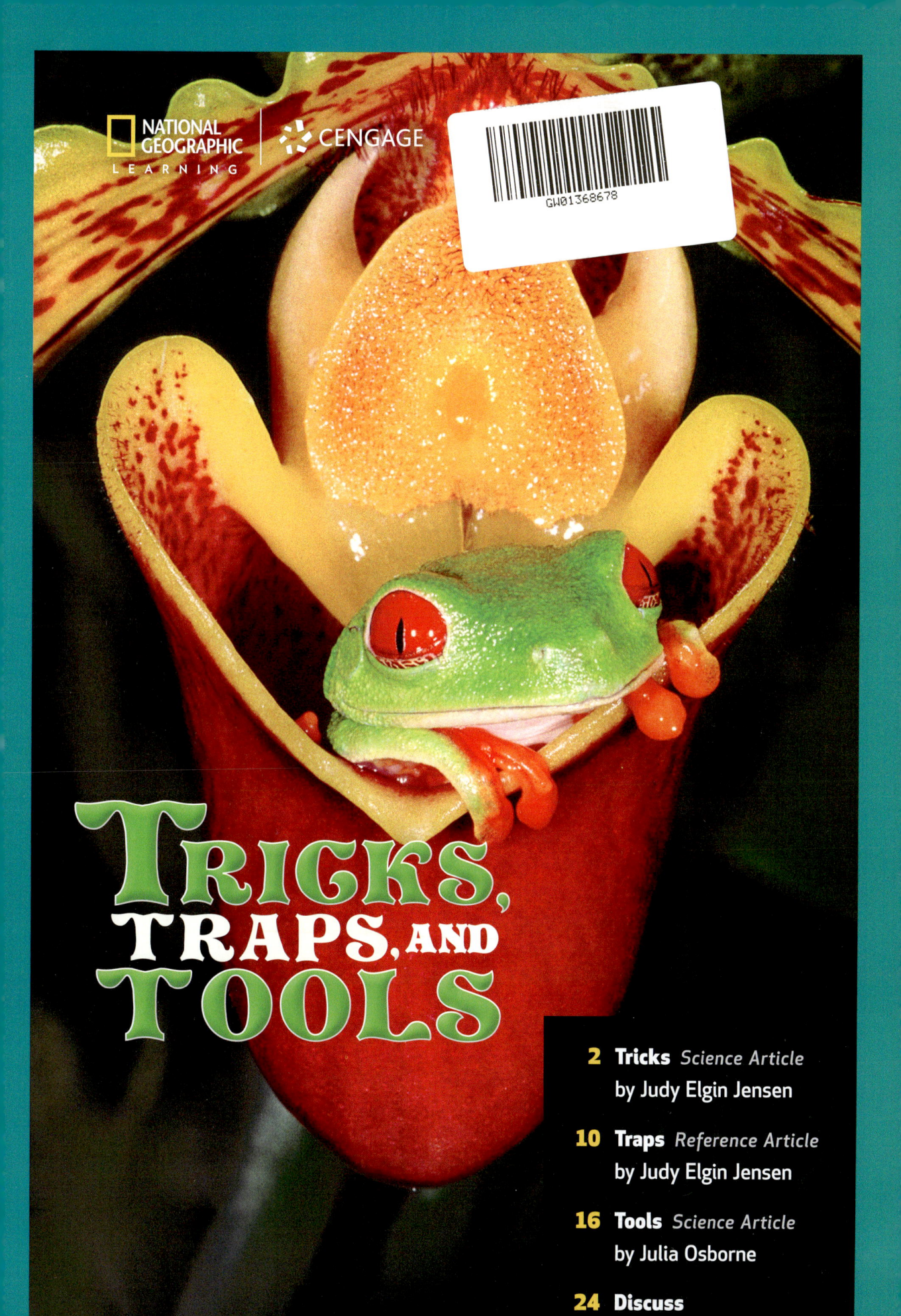

2 Tricks *Science Article*
by Judy Elgin Jensen

10 Traps *Reference Article*
by Judy Elgin Jensen

16 Tools *Science Article*
by Julia Osborne

24 Discuss

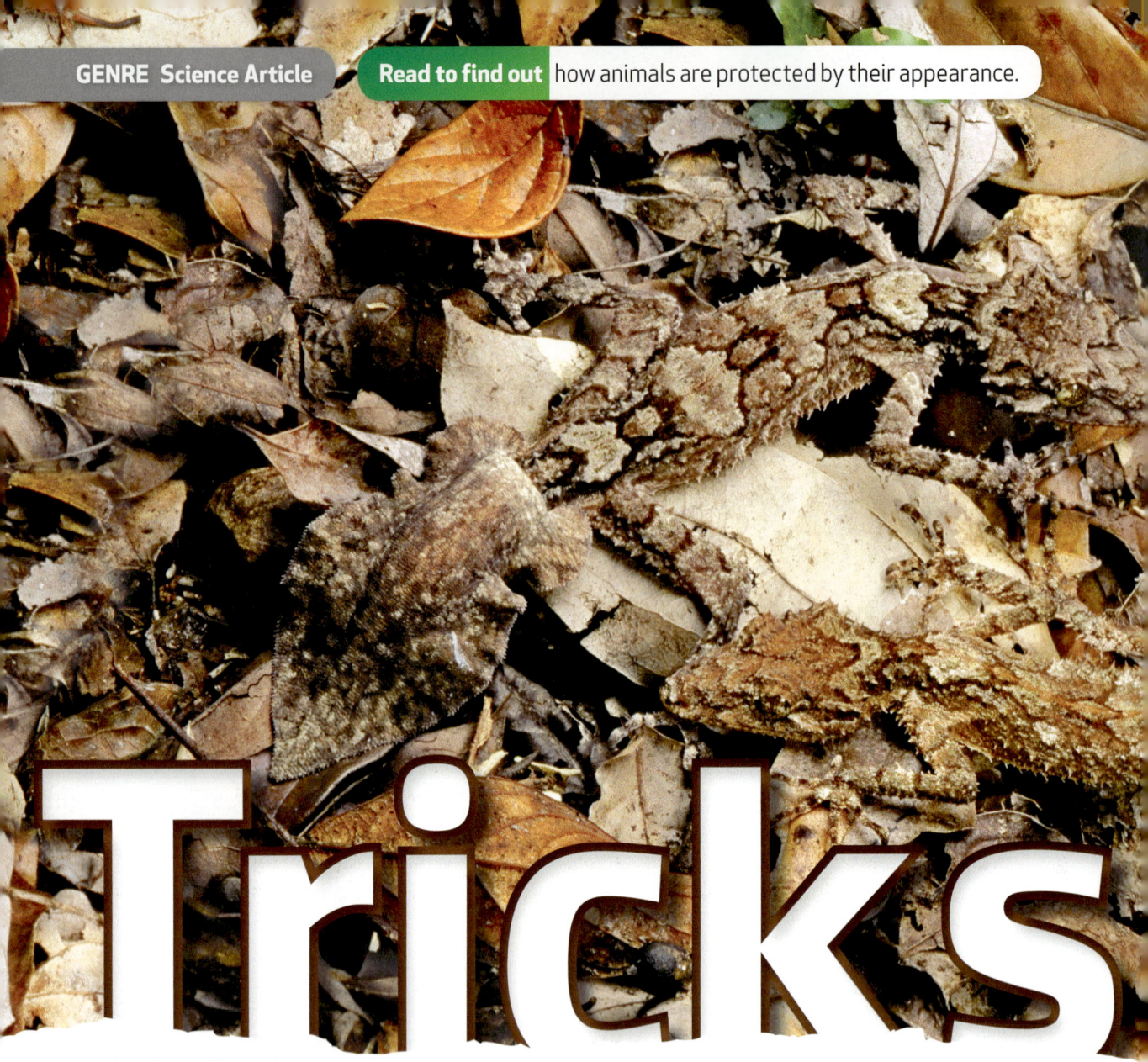

GENRE Science Article   Read to find out how animals are protected by their appearance.

Tricks

by Judy Elgin Jensen

Imagine walking in a rain forest in Queensland, Australia. Dead brown leaves litter the ground. But look closely. Are they all *really* leaves? In nature, what you see is not always what you get!

Among the leaves are several leaf-tailed geckos. They are colored and shaped like leaves. Even their tails look like leaves. These geckos are very still, waiting to attack insects. **Predators** that would like to eat the geckos cannot see them easily.

2

How many leaf-tailed geckos can you find? The background has been lightened to make it easier to see one of them.

On the ground, the colors of the leaf-tailed geckos are similar. But soon they will scamper away, climbing up different trees. There each gecko's coloring will change to shades of brown or green. Then they will look different from one another. They are all the same kind of gecko, though.

Have you found the leaf-tailed geckos yet? If you look closely, you can find three of them.

Hiding in Plain Sight

Like leaf-tailed geckos, many animals use **camouflage** for protection. Their skins, shells, fur, or feathers look like their surroundings. It is hard for a predator to see an animal that is the color and shape of things around it. Some predators use camouflage to hide from their prey. If their prey come close, they catch and eat them.

Jagged Ambush Bug
Where it lives: Eastern North America
What's special: This bug sits on flowers, especially goldenrod. When an insect lands, the bug grabs it and kills it with poison. The bug often attacks insects larger than itself. Look for the bug's green and brown body.

Malaysian Orchid Mantis
Where it lives: Rain forests in Malaysia
What's special: This mantis looks like an orchid blossom. Like some orchids, some mantises are pink or purple. To find the mantis, look for its dark eyes.

Soft Coral Crab
Where it lives: Coral reefs near Indonesia
What's special: This crab lives among coral polyps. To find the crab, look for its spiny legs with pink stripes.

5

Looking Dangerous

Not all animals survive by camouflage. Dangerous animals often have bright colors or patterns that make them stand out. Predators avoid animals with warning colors. Some harmless animals have colors and patterns that mimic, or copy, those of dangerous animals. These copycats stay safe through **mimicry.**

Model: Plain Tiger Butterfly

The plain tiger caterpillar eats leaves that make the adult taste bad to predators. The adults can also release bad-smelling fluids.

Mimic: Danaid Eggfly Butterfly

The female danaid eggfly looks like the plain tiger, does not taste bad. Predators mistake it for the bad-tasting plain tiger and stay away.

Model: Yellowjacket

The yellowjacket wasp can give predators a painful sting.

Mimic: Yellowjacket Hover Fly

This harmless hover fly looks like a yellowjacket. It sounds like one, too.

Model: Coral Snake

The poisonous coral snake has bands of yellow, black, and red. Like a speeding red fire truck, its bands say, "Watch out!" The scarlet king snake is not poisonous. But it has bands like those of the coral snake. Predators know coral snakes can make them sick. So they avoid all banded snakes, including the scarlet king snake.

Mimic: Scarlet King Snake

Confusing Predators

Some animals confuse predators or scare them away. They may puff themselves up to look bigger. Their markings may look like a larger animal's markings.

Io Moth
When startled, the io moth spreads its wings (above). On its back wings are large black eyespots. To predators, the eyespots look like the eyes of an owl (to the right).

8

Puss Moth Caterpillar
The caterpillar of the European puss moth is green like a leaf. When it is startled, it pulls its head into its body and rears up. A predator sees a big red "mouth." If that doesn't scare the predator away, the caterpillar's two tails squirt acid at it!

Some animals use camouflage to hide from predators. Other animals have bright colors and patterns that keep predators away. Whatever the strategy, the goal is always survival.

Check In How does mimicry protect an animal from predators?

GENRE Reference Article   Read to find out how some plants get nutrients in an unusual way.

Traps

by Judy Elgin Jensen

A frog hops among the sticky sundew plants. It never suspects that the plants are dangerous. Oops! Too close. Now the frog is stuck to a plant. The sticky liquid of the sundew will smother the frog. Then the frog will be turned into soup for the sundew plant.

Plants use sunlight to make their own food. Plants also need **nutrients**, such as nitrogen, from the soil. In many swamps and bogs, the soil does not contain enough nutrients. **Carnivorous plants** in these places get nitrogen by trapping small animals.

The tentacles of a sundew fold down to trap prey.

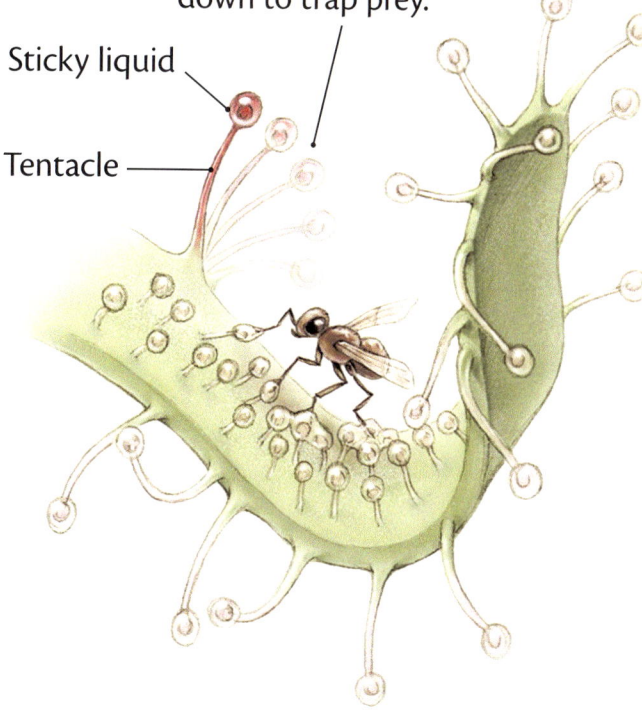

Sticky liquid

Tentacle

This frog is caught in a sticky sundew plant.

Sundews

There are about 150 kinds of sundew plants. Some are as tiny as a dime. Others are taller than you! Some sundew leaves grow in a circle, and others grow upward in stalks. Thick hairs, or tentacles, cover the leaves. Sticky liquid on each tentacle traps and digests animals.

Bladderworts

A netlike plant covered with tiny "bubbles" floats in a pond. A small animal swims by and touches trigger hairs on a bubble. WHOOSH! The water around the animal is sucked into the bubble. The water carries the animal with it. That's no bubble. It's a trap!

The trap slams shut. Digestive juices fill the trap. Goodbye tiny animal.

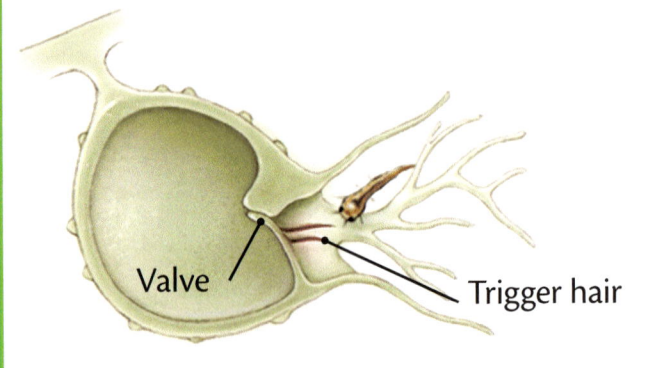

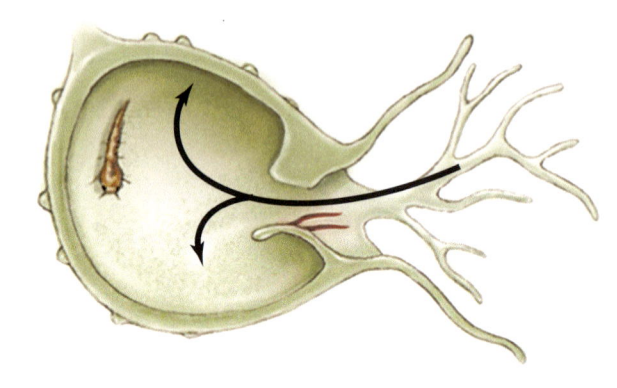

Valve — Trigger hair

∧ The bladderwort pumps water out of its trap. If an animal touches a trigger hair, the trap opens. Water rushes in. The animal goes in, too.

< Bladderworts don't have roots to get nutrients from soil. Instead they get their nutrients from tiny animals.

Venus Flytraps

Venus flytraps capture small animals that creep across their leaves. There are trigger hairs on the inside of each leaf. If an animal touches the trigger hairs, the leaf snaps shut and traps the animal. After about seven days, the trapped animal is digested. Then the leaf opens again, ready for its next meal.

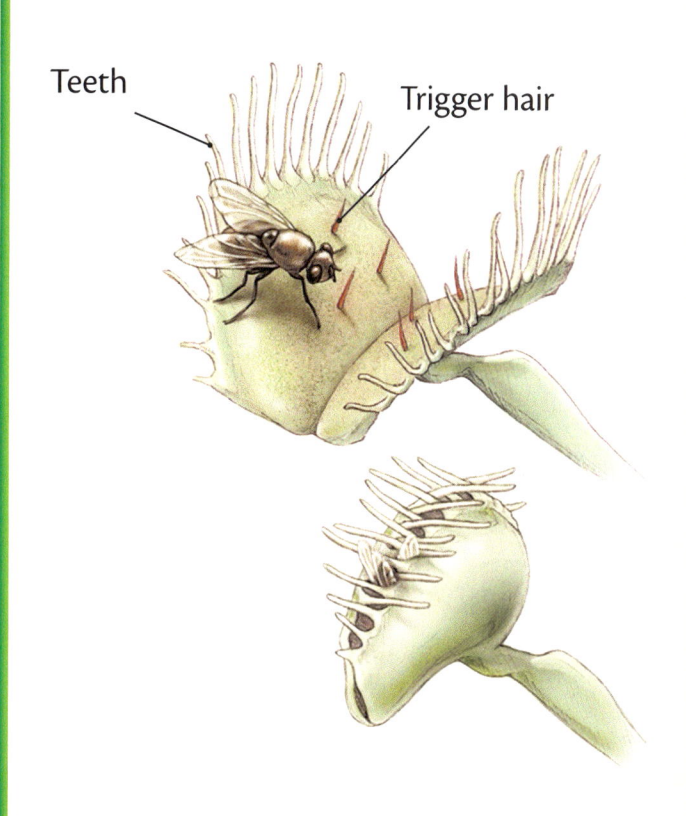

Teeth

Trigger hair

⌄ When an insect walks across a Venus flytrap leaf, it touches the trigger hairs. That causes the two halves of the leaf to snap shut.

Pitcher Plants

A pitcher-shaped leaf gives off a sweet smell of nectar. An ant leans in to sip the nectar. Soon the ant is sliding down the slippery inside of the pitcher. At the bottom is a pool of water and digestive fluid. There the ant drowns. The ant's body breaks down, releasing nutrients that the plant needs.

> As the ant tries to crawl out of the pitcher, it runs into hairs that point downward. The hairs act as spears and keep the ant in the pool.

- Lid
- Slippery rim
- Waxy zone
- Digestive fluid

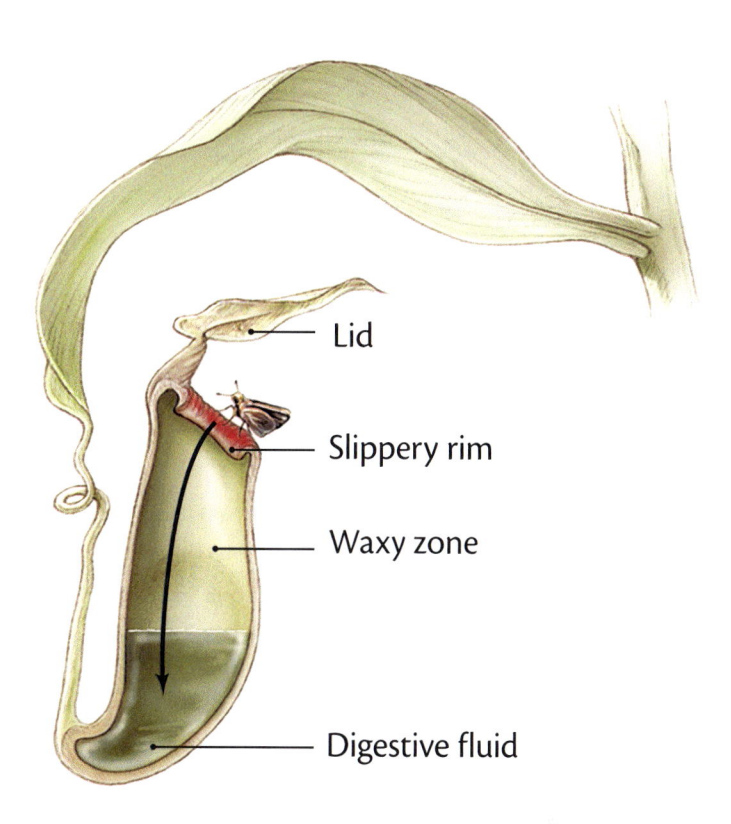

Carnivorous plants thrive where most other plants cannot get enough nutrients. Their specialized structures trap and digest small animals. This gives the plants the nutrients they need.

Yum. Bug juice.

Check In How does the leaf of a pitcher plant trap an ant?

GENRE Science Article   Read to find out some ways that animals use tools.

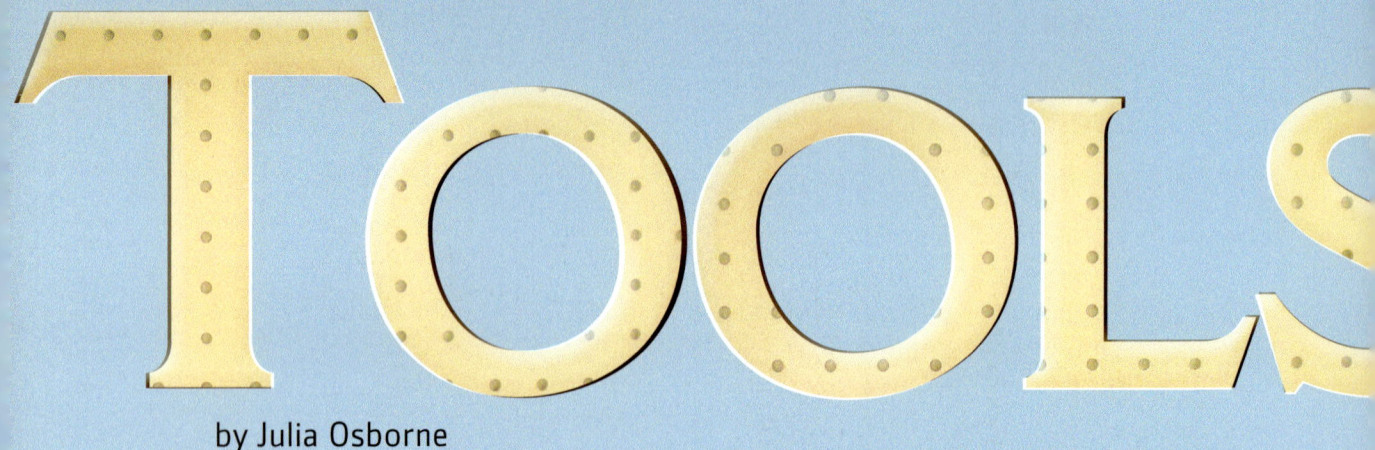

TOOLS

by Julia Osborne

What kinds of tools do you use? You probably use many. They may be simple, such as spoons, or complex, such as computers. Tools are objects used to carry out a task. Humans use many different tools.

Scientists once thought only humans had enough brainpower to use tools. But that idea is changing.

For example, the Egyptian vulture likes to eat eggs. If an egg is small, the vulture picks it up and drops it. When the egg breaks, the vulture slurps up the insides. Ostrich eggs are too big for the vulture to pick up. The vulture uses a stone as a tool. It throws the stone at the egg to break it. Then it eats its meal.

Read on to learn how some animals use objects to perform a task or change their environment.

⟨ **An Eyptian vulture drops a stone on an egg.**

▽ The sound of rushing water triggers a special behavior in a beaver. It builds a dam. The dam holds back the water, making a pond.